LOVE EARTH

The Beauty Makeover

By Shelly Nielsen
Illustrated by Terry Boles

Published by Abdo & Daughters, 6535 Cecilia Circle, Edina, Minnesota 55439.

Library bound edition distributed by Rockbottom Books, Pentagon Tower, P.O. Box 36036, Minneapolis, Minnesota 55435.

Edited by Julie Berg

LIBRARY OF CONGRESS CATALOGING-IN-PUBLICATION DATA
Nielsen, Shelly, 1958-
    Love Earth: the beauty makeover / written by Shelly Nielsen : [edited by Julie Berg].
        p. cm. -- (Target Earth)
    Includes bibliographical references.
    Summary: Describes some of the problems facing the Earth and outlines things that we can all do to combat pollution.
        ISBN 1-56239-198-4 (lib. bdg.)
        1. Environmental protection -- Citizen participation -- Juvenile literature. 2. Pollution -- Juvenile literature. [1. Pollution. 2. Environmental protection.] I. Berg, Julie. II Title. III. Series.
    TD171.7.N54   1993
    363.7'0525--dc20
                                                93-18954
                                                CIP

Thanks To The Trees From Which This Recycled Paper Was First Made.

The beautiful Earth was in trouble. Just look! Pollution
everywhere. The whole world seemed sad and sick.
Something had to be done—and right away, too! But I
was just one small person. What could one kid do?

Cough! Cough! Once the air was sweet and clean.
Then it became dirty. So this is what I did...

I used a fan instead of an air conditioner.

I made a poster that said, "Keep Our Air Clean!"

I rode my bike instead of riding in a car.

When we all work together, doesn't the air smell sweet?

Once the Earth's waters were clear. Then there was garbage in the rivers. Yech! Junk in the lakes. Trash in the sea. So this is what I did...

I helped my Mom and Dad write letters to companies.
"Please don't put chemicals and other pollution in the water,"
we wrote.

I grabbed a bag and picked up trash on the beach.

When we all work together, doesn't the water look clean?

Once the trees were strong and tall. Then many beautiful forests were cut down. So this is what I did...

I didn't waste paper towels, napkins, or tissues.

I saved paper bags instead of throwing them away.

I planted a tree!

I told everyone to use less paper.

When we all work together, look how the trees grow thick and tall.

Once the Earth was clean. Then the streets became filled with garbage. Gross! So this is what I did...

I helped Daddy recharge batteries instead of throwing them away.

At home, I used rags instead of paper towels.

I recycled cans, plastic, and bottles. I joined a clean-up team that picked up all the trash in our neighborhood.

When we all work together, look how the litter disappears.

Once insects crept and crawled on the Earth. Then chemicals killed the V.I.B.'s (very important bugs)! So this is what I did...

I saved a bug's life! I moved a beetle off the sidewalk so it wouldn't get squashed.

I stopped using bug spray. It's poison!

"Hey, everyone," I said. "We need insect friends."

When we all work together, people and bugs can live side by side on Earth!

Help! Once the birds flew carefree. Then pollution made them sick. So this is what I did...

I picked up all the garbage so the birds wouldn't eat it and get sick.

I made a birdbath to put in the backyard.

I planted sunflowers just for my bird friends. When the seeds are ready, the birds will have a seed feast.

When we all work together, the air is filled with birds and songs!

Once the animals were safe on the Earth. Then they were in danger! So this is what I did...

I helped Mom cut apart plastic six-pack rings so they wouldn't get stuck around an animal's neck.

I would never wear a fur coat.

I showed my friends how to be kind to animals.

When we all work together, the animals are safe and happy again.

Once the plants were strong and green. Then they were full of chemicals. Yuk! So this is what I did...

I grew plants all by myself.

I learned to make compost to feed the garden.

I didn't use chemicals or poisons.

When we all work together, look how the healthy plants grow.

Once the Earth was sad and sick. Then everyone worked
together. So this is what we did...

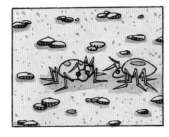

We cleaned up the air.

We cleaned the water.

We planted more trees.

We gathered the trash.

We cared for the bugs.

We helped the birds.

We loved the animals.

We grew healthy plants.

 And when we all worked together...

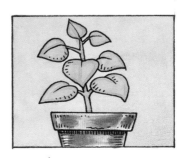

...we saved the Earth. What a beautiful world!

Other things we can do to keep the Earth beautiful:

• Buy soft drinks in returnable bottles.

• Always turn off lights when you leave a room.

• Plant a tree. Trees remove carbon dioxide from the air and add oxygen.

• Ride your bike or walk whenever possible.

• Fix leaky faucets.

• Take a shower instead of a bath. Showers use one-third less water than baths.

• Set up a bird feeder in your backyard.

• Join a wildlife organization such as the National Wildlife Federation.

Target Earth™ Commitment

At Target, we're committed to the environment. We show this commitment not only through our own internal efforts but also through the programs we sponsor in the communities where we do business.

Our commitment to children and the environment began when we became the Founding International Sponsor for Kids for Saving Earth, a non-profit environmental organization for kids. We helped launch the program in 1989 and supported its growth to three-quarters of a million club members in just three years.

Our commitment to children's environmental education led to the development of an environmental curriculum called Target Earth™, aimed at getting kids involved in their education and in their world.

In addition, we worked with Abdo & Daughters Publishing to develop the Target Earth™ Earthmobile, an environmental science library on wheels that can be used in libraries, or rolled from classroom to classroom.

Target believes that the children are our future and the future of our planet. Through education, they will save the world!

Minneapolis-based Target Stores is an upscale discount department store chain of 517 stores in 33 states coast-to-coast, and is the largest division of Dayton Hudson Corporation, one of the nation's leading retailers.